All Things Considered

A comedy

Ben Brown

Samuel French — London
New York - Toronto - Hollywood

ALL THINGS CONSIDERED

First presented in the McCarthy Theatre at the Stephen
Joseph Theatre, Scarborough, on 14th November, 1996,
with the following cast:

David	Christopher Godwin
Ronnie	Michael Lumsden
Bob	Neil Percival
Laura	Holly Hayes
Tom	Timothy Kightley
Margaret	Susie Blake
Joanna	Jane Slavin

The play was directed by Alan Strachan
Designed by Michael Holt
Lighting by Paul Towson

This production transferred to the Hampstead Theatre,
London, on 9th June, 1997, with the same cast.

The action takes place in the living-room of David
Freeman's college flat

"There is but one truly serious philosophical problem, and that is suicide. Judging whether life is or is not worth living amounts to answering the fundamental question of philosophy."

Albert Camus, *The Myth of Sisyphus*

"Be philosophical. Don't think about it."

Woman on a bus

For Jenny and Jenny

With thanks to Michael Codron
who commissioned this play
and saw it through to production

ACT I

The living-room of David Freeman's college flat

Up stage, large windows with heavy dark curtains. There is a door to the communal hall UL, a door to the bedroom and bathroom DL, and a door to the kitchen and cellar UR. Bookcases on all the walls. In the bookcase L is a stereo. Left, a sofa and, down stage, a small table with a bottle of whisky and some glasses. Facing the sofa R is an easy chair. Further right, a desk with an antique upright chair. On the desk, a computer, a telephone with an answering machine, a lamp, a silver-framed photograph of an elderly woman and an open book

Life is So Peculiar, *sung by Louis Armstrong and Louis Jordan plays as the audience settles. Lights up on the stage. The window curtains are closed and the room is lit by various lamps*

David, forty-nine and slightly worn both in features and dress, sits in the easy chair holding a glass of whisky

The music fades

He gets up, goes over to the drinks table and generously refills his glass. He takes the glass and switches off the lamps one by one as he goes to the desk. The only remaining source of light is the desk lamp. He closes the book and lays it face down. He sits down. Pause. He puts the photograph face down

Pause

Decisively, he opens a drawer. He takes out a small bottle, a transparent plastic bag and a large elastic band. He puts the plastic bag on his head and secures it with the elastic band so that he wears it like a chef's hat. He then unscrews the bottle and pours pills on to the desk. He picks up two and prepares to swallow

The phone rings. He stops. He waits for it to stop. It doesn't. He switches the answering machine on. The phone stops ringing. We hear David's recorded message from the answering machine: "Hello. This is David Freeman. I'm

afraid I'm out at the moment but if you wait for the tone you can leave a
message and I'll call you back later."

The tone

Ronnie (*on the line*) Hi, David. How's life?

Pause

What a stupid thing to say... Listen, I've got a bit of a problem...
Something personal. Well, I say personal. It may be professional too.
Depends how you look at it. Sort of personal-professional. I don't know.
I'm too ... personally involved. God, I hate these machines. Where are
you?

David reaches out for the phone but draws back again

Sorry. It's just I need some independent advice. And you're the only person
I can trust. So get in touch. ...Thanks, David. You're a pal...

David fingers the receiver indecisively

I don't know what I'd do without you.

He picks up the phone

David What is it, Ronnie?
Ronnie David! You're in!
David Yes. What's the problem?
Ronnie Have you heard what I've been saying?
David Yes.
Ronnie You mean you were there all the time?
David Yes.
Ronnie ...I suspected you of being one of those people.

A little pause

David What's the problem, Ronnie?
Ronnie Is it still on?
David What?
Ronnie Never mind. I'll come round.
David Ah...
Ronnie Won't be long.

David Actually, Ronnie——

We hear the dialling tone

Ronnie...? Ronnie!

He looks in agitation at the receiver

Bugger.

He puts it down, picks it up again and starts dialling. A knock at the door. He puts the phone down. Another knock. He hurriedly puts the pills back in the bottle. Louder knocks

(*Calling*) I'm coming!

He puts the pill bottle into the drawer and goes to the door, but then realizes he's still got the plastic bag on his head. He takes it off and puts it in the drawer. He opens the door

Bob, carrying a tool kit, walks past him into the room

Bob Morning, Professor. Just got up, have you? That's the life.
David Who are you?
Bob I'm Bob. Lovely day out. Shall I draw your curtains? (*He draws the curtains*)

The room is filled with light. David squints

That's better. Now just tell me where the mains are and I'll leave you in peace.
David What?
Bob The mains. Just tell me where they are.
David Why?
Bob Well, I can't do your rewiring without knowing where the mains are, can I?
David Rewiring?
Bob ...Don't tell me you didn't know?
David I didn't.
Bob But you must have seen the notice? There's one up in the lodge.
David I haven't noticed any notice. What rewiring?
Bob The whole college. Hasn't been rewired for fifty years. Could be dangerous.

David Could it…?

Bob And with all this wood panelling…

David Look, it happens to be rather a big day for me. Couldn't you do it tomorrow?

Bob Sorry. Not possible. I've done all the others except you and upstairs, and since you and upstairs are on the same circuit, and the mains are down here, I can't do upstairs until I've started on you. See what I mean?

David What if I don't want my rooms rewired?

Bob Ah, well, technically they're college rooms. You see, it's the insurance. They've demanded it. Anyway, we wouldn't want a professor of philosophy put in danger, would we? Now. Where are the mains? Through here? (*He indicates off* R)

David Yes. In the cellar— Look, how long will this take?

Bob You just carry on, Professor. You won't know I'm here.

Bob goes off whistling Life is So Peculiar

David has the look of a man whose plans have been disrupted. He goes to the desk and puts the photograph back up

Laura, an attractive young American carrying an A4-size envelope, appears in the doorway. She watches David for a moment before he sees her

Laura Ah… I wasn't planning that we should meet yet. I was just going to put this through your letter box. Actually, you don't seem to have a letter box, do you? Of course, I could have left it at the porter's lodge. But I wanted to make sure you got it as soon as possible, seeing as this is rather last minute. It's my paper. For this afternoon. I'm handing round advance copies. I don't know about you but I always find it hard to take things in aurally. I mean, when people speak for any length of time I find them very difficult to follow.

A little pause

David What are you talking about?

Laura You too, huh? I'll say it again. This is a copy of the paper I'm giving this afternoon.

David You're giving a paper?

Laura You've got it. I'm Laura Booth. From Berkeley. My résumé's enclosed. (*She holds out the envelope*) Kidneys.

David What?

Laura That's the subject of my paper. What's yours?

David What makes you think I'm giving a paper?
Laura Well, aren't you?
David Not as far as I know. God, I hope not.
Laura Sorry, I just assumed... I mean seeing that it's right up your alley.
David What is?
Laura The symposium.
David What symposium?
Laura The one this afternoon. Medical ethics.
David I'm afraid you're under a misapprehension. I'm neither aware of nor attending any symposium this afternoon about medical ethics or any other subject.

Pause

Laura You're not?
David No.

Pause

Laura You are Professor Freeman?
David Yes.
Laura Well, that's something I've got right. Lucky I brought this around then. (*She offers him the envelope*) I'd still like to hear your comments. If you have the time. I'm a great admirer of your work.
David Thank you.
Laura You're welcome.

He takes the paper from her

David If I have the time.
Laura Great. I'll come back later then. Say, lunchtime?
David Actually, I'm rather tied up today.
Laura OK. Another time.

Pause. He expects her to go

When's good for you? I'm easy.
David Ah...
Laura Tomorrow morning?
David You see——
Laura Tomorrow lunch?
David The thing is——
Laura Or are the evenings better for you?

David I really don't think I'll have time.
Laura How about now?
David Now?
Laura I could just outline my argument briefly and then you can tell me what you think. (*Little pause*) I'd really appreciate it.
David ...Well... I suppose I do have a few minutes to kill...
Laura Great.

Pause

David Perhaps you'd like some coffee?
Laura Thank you.
David ...You're welcome.

David goes off to the kitchen

Laura takes her coat off and hangs it over the back of the sofa. She heads for the bookshelf L. She takes out a book and begins to read

David enters

Laura "I believe that when I die I shall rot, and nothing of my ego will survive."

David stops. She shows him the cover

Bertrand Russell.
David Ah...
Laura (*closing the book*) Beautiful.
David ...Sugar?
Laura What?
David Do you take sugar?
Laura Oh. No, thanks.
David Milk?
Laura Please.

David goes off again

Laura replaces the book and looks around the room

David enters with the coffee. He's surprised to find her now looking through the bookshelf on the other side of the room

Nice place you've got here. Do you live alone?
David Yes. (*He gives her the coffee*)
Laura Thank you. (*She goes over to the antique upright chair*) I like this old chair. (*She sits in it*)
David It was my mother's.
Laura Oh...
David Of course, it's not real.

Laura is puzzled. She looks at the chair

Laura I'm sorry?
David The coffee.

They smile

Tell me about your paper.
Laura Right... It's about whether people should be allowed to sell their kidneys.
David Yes. A tricky one.
Laura I don't think so.
David Well, I know what you mean. Turning kidneys into commodities does seem pretty objectionable.
Laura No. I mean, I think we should encourage a market in organs. Why not? People wouldn't sell their kidneys unless they needed the money more. A market will create an optimal organ distribution.

David looks unconvinced

I know what you're thinking. You're thinking people should donate, not sell. Hey, let's foster altruism! Like with blood. But when it comes to giving away a kidney, altruism seems to be a little thin on the ground. Not surprising really, when you come to think about it. But, of course, if more people carried donor cards... I mean, surely when you're dead you can spare a kidney? (*Little pause*) Do you carry a donor card?
David (*surprised*) What?
Laura I'm sorry. That's a personal question. On second thoughts, perhaps it would be better if I just left the paper with you. I'm more detached in my writing.
David Very well ... but I really don't think I'll have time.
Laura I'll take a chance. Anyway, I'd rather talk about you.

David looks alarmed. She sips her coffee

So Professor, what are you up to?
David How do you mean?
Laura If you're so busy, you must be working on something.
David Ah...actually...no.
Laura Oh...
David But I've just published a book.
Laura Great.
David It's called *Matters of Life and Death*.
Laura Good title. I saw a movie called that.
David Ah. No. That's *A Matter of Life and Death*. Singular.
Laura Oh, right. Yes, I remember. A guy falls in love with a girl over the radio just before his plane's about to crash. He's English, she's American. He's got no parachute but he doesn't want to burn so he jumps to his certain death. Only they make a mistake in heaven so he doesn't die after all. (*Little pause*) What's the name of that actor?
David David Niven.
Laura (*nodding*) David Niven. I like him. Hey, your name's David, isn't it?
David Yes.

She nods

Laura Sorry, you were telling me about your book.
David Yes. It's about abortion, capital punishment, euthanasia and suicide.
Laura Sounds fun.
David The basics of applied ethics. My aim is to discuss all these mortal questions together so as to give a coherent and fresh restatement of the liberal position. My premise is that the ultimate choice between life and death should always be left to the person whose life and autonomy is in question.
Laura And you conclude, abortion OK, euthanasia OK, suicide OK, capital punishment *not* OK?
David (*taken aback*) Yes...
Laura OK. I'm with you. Except on capital punishment.
David You're in favour of capital punishment?
Laura Well, not as it currently operates in certain states back home—where it actually means if you've got the capital you can avoid the punishment— but in theory, yes. The thing is, you've got to look at it from the recycling angle.
David The recycling angle?
Laura Yeh. If the organs of murderers and rapists were used for transplant operations, why, then counting the kidneys, the liver, the heart, and lungs, the corneas, the bone marrow ... well, just one death penalty could yield

as much as five, six, seven, eight better lives. In future, maybe more. You know, right now in Pittsburgh they're working on bowels.

David Really...

Laura So you see, by organ recycling, serial killers could become serial life-savers, which has a nice kind of justice to it, don't you think?

David Well, it's ... an original idea.

Laura It better be. It's the subject of my doctorate. Actually, my thesis has been overtaken by events. In China they now time executions to facilitate transplant surgery. Life imitates philosophy. But speaking of abortion, I'm already acquainted with your '71 article.

David Ah... (*he realizes he doesn't remember*) '71 you say?

Laura Yeh, I love that article. I mean, the abortion debate so often gets stuck on the issue of whether or not a foetus is a human being. But you were able to move the debate on and say, OK, even if it is a human being—even if it's a person, just like you or me—we don't have the right to sit in someone else's womb for nine months!

David (*embarrassed*) Yes, well——

Laura Or, alternatively, if the foetus isn't a person—because it hasn't got a character and rationality and self-consciousness and all that stuff—then it isn't a person after birth either. At least, not right away. So, logically, infanticide's OK too.

David Hmn...

Laura Not many would have had the courage to make that point.

David Actually, I've retreated somewhat from that position.

Laura Really? I don't think you should.

A little pause

What's that book you're reading?

David What?

She picks up the book on the desk

Laura I'm sorry but I just have to know what people are reading...

David Ah...

Laura (*surprised*) *Final Exit.*

David ...For my book.

Laura *The Practicalities of Self-Deliverance.*

David ...I think one needs to know the practicalities before one can construct the theory.

Laura Right... Actually, I've heard of this book. Back home it caused a real controversy. They thought we'd all go putting plastic bags over our heads.

(*She laughs*) Hey, you shouldn't leave books like this lying around. People will get the wrong idea.

David Yes. It was careless of me. (*He puts the book in a drawer*)

Laura But I thought you'd finished your book?

David hesitates

The door opens and Ronnie enters talking

Ronnie David, I'm sorry to interrupt your work but—— (*He sees Laura, stops and gawps at her*) Ah...

Laura Hi.

Ronnie (*smitten*) Hello... David, I'm not interrupting anything important, am I?

David Not at all. Laura just dropped in for a philosophical chat. She's from California.

Laura Are you a philosopher too?

Ronnie Me? No, English.

Laura (*losing interest*) Oh... Anyway, it's been nice talking to you, Professor. (*She holds out her hand*)

David (*shaking her hand*) And you.

Laura I can't tempt you?

David What?

Laura To the symposium.

David Ah...

Ronnie Symposium?

David Kidneys.

Ronnie Oh... (*He looks puzzled*)

David 'Fraid I can't.

Laura Pity. (*She collects her things*) Maybe I'll come fill you in later.

Laura exits

Ronnie Nice girl.

David Yes.

Ronnie Very nice.

David What can I do for you, Ronnie?

Ronnie How about a whisky?

David It's rather early, isn't it?

Ronnie That's a bit rich coming from you. I see you've started already. (*He indicates the whisky on the desk and gives a knowing smile*)

David goes to the drinks table. Pause

You know, I've never done it with an American.
David Actually, Ronnie, I didn't know. But knowing you, I'm surprised.
Ronnie I've done it with a Canadian. But that's not quite the same. Screw an American and you screw the world.

David hands him a drink

Thanks. (*He drinks*) Have you ever done it with an American?
David Ronnie, I thought you were in urgent need of my independent advice.
Ronnie Yes. Sorry. I was just sort of... (*he gestures with his glass*) circling in on it. You see, we're already, as the Americans say, in the right ball park.

David thinks

David I see.
Ronnie Do you? Oh dear. You know me too well.
David You're up to your old tricks again.
Ronnie Oh, don't say it like that.
David Like what?
Ronnie In that disapproving paternalistic tone. I mean I've tried. I've really tried. Every year. I say to myself. Look, Ronnie. No more students. It always ends in tears. So I sit there as they read out their essays on Lawrence or whoever. And they're banging on about Freud. And finding phallic symbols all over the place. Never mind the symbol, the real thing's at full throttle right under their noses. But I'd been doing so well. So well. I mean, it's been three years now, since ... since ... what was her name?
David Emily.
Ronnie Emily. Yes. She was the last. Well, she was going to be the last. But then ... well, it was those black stockings.
David My ex-wife used to wear black stockings.
Ronnie Did she? Yes, I've always had this thing about black stockings. Don't know why. I can resist everything except black stockings. I mean, any other colour would have been fine ... you'd think black would go out of fashion, wouldn't you? But no, first tutorial this term and those black stockings walked into the room. Don't look down, I said to myself. Whatever you do, don't look down... But I always do.
David Mmm. Weakness of the will. Really, Ronnie, you know you shouldn't sleep with students. Times have changed. It's no longer regarded as a perk of the job. It's now considered a breach of trust. An abuse of power and position. And your academic reputation isn't going to save you. One hears stories of unmarked essays, drunken tutorials——
Ronnie That was once...
David And when did you last publish?

Ronnie Nineteen eighty-one…
David Precisely.

Ronnie reflects

Ronnie *Images of Defloration in Medieval Literature*. A brilliant article.
David So the seeds of decline were there all along…
Ronnie It's true I've rather lost interest in the work.
David Yes… Well, I suggest you lose interest in this student or you may find yourself up in front of the disciplinary committee.
Ronnie I know that.
David Yes, you know and yet you persist. Weakness of the will. Personally, I can't understand it. Once I've decided on the rational course of action, I pursue it. It's a philosophical problem as to how anyone can do otherwise.
Ronnie Maybe it's just my libido will is stronger than my professional will.
David Well then, that makes you no more than an animal. A mere slave to your primitive instincts.
Ronnie But aren't we all like that?
David So Hume thought. But I disagree. We can overcome those instincts. If we want to. We are different from other animals.
Ronnie Really? How?
David There have been many theories. For example, that only we have language. That only we laugh. That only we live with an awareness of death. That only we commit suicide—but this is beside the point. What's so special this time? No-one else knows, do they?
Ronnie No.
David So, what's the problem?
Ronnie They will do soon.
David Why? Is she threatening to tell people?
Ronnie Not exactly.
David What then?
Ronnie …She seems to have got herself pregnant.

Pause

David I see. How did that happen?
Ronnie How do you think?
David I mean, weren't you … wearing anything?
Ronnie Well, of course I wasn't, was I? Otherwise she wouldn't be up the bloody spout, would she?
David No. She wouldn't.

Pause

Ronnie Look, actually, she's a Catholic. She doesn't believe in contraception.
David But she believes in premarital sex?
Ronnie What? No. Of course not, but...
David You're irresistible?
Ronnie Yes. But that's not the point. The point is she wants to have it. The baby, I mean.
David Mm... Oh dear.

Pause

Ronnie Look, David, you don't think you can talk her out of it, do you?
David Talk her out of it?
Ronnie Yes.
David You mean persuade her to have an abortion?
Ronnie Well ... yes. I mean it just isn't fair that she should have it. Our sex life was supposed to be recreational not procreational. And it's obvious she doesn't really want it. She just has ... irrational scruples based on some hangover of religious belief. I tried to tell her it was all a load of mumbo jumbo.

There is a knock at the door

David (*calling*) Yes.
Ronnie I mean, who believes in God these days?

Tom, dog-collared but otherwise informally dressed, pokes his head round the door

Ronnie chokes on his whisky

Tom Are you all right, Ronnie?
Ronnie Just got a bit of a cough.
David What can I do for you, Tom?
Tom Oh ... nothing urgent. I'll pop back later.

Tom exits

Ronnie Christ, you don't think he heard, do you?
David Well, what does it matter? So you don't believe in God.
Ronnie No, I mean about this girl.
David Oh... No, of course not.
Ronnie Because you know what he's like. He'd go straight to the Dean.

David He couldn't possibly have heard.

Ronnie Perhaps you're right. I'm just being paranoid. But you will talk to her, won't you? I'm sure you could overcome her with your philosophical argument.

David In my experience religious belief is rarely overcome by philosophical argument. Anyway, I can't.

Ronnie Why not?

David On moral grounds. It's entirely a matter for her.

Ronnie Mmm. I thought you'd say that. There's only one thing to do then. Marry her.

David is surprised

David Ronnie, I don't like to put a dampener on things but, as a friend, I think I should point out that you're already married.

Ronnie Yes…

David To someone else.

Ronnie I know.

David To someone else, indeed, who has borne you three children—and wait a minute, isn't Jean…?

Ronnie stares into his glass

I see. So you are now expecting children by two different women.

Ronnie Actually, Jean being pregnant is partly the cause of this.

David What?

Ronnie She loses interest in sex. Well, not at first. Quite the opposite. But for the last couple of months she has. Apparently, that's what happens in the second trimester. Anyway, you know me. I can't do without it. I'd go mad. So that, on top of a pair of black stockings…

David Ronnie, what surprises me is not your adultery but that you can seriously suggest marrying the girl.

Ronnie Why not? All I need is a divorce. And they could hardly sack me for getting a student pregnant if I then did the honourable thing and married her. You see. It all makes perfect sense.

Pause

David Right, Ronnie, you obviously have the practicalities of the situation well in hand. If you wish to end one marriage and start another I really don't see how I can stop you. Or indeed help. Except to warn you that, in my experience, divorce is a pretty miserable affair. And very expensive. And we didn't have children. And it takes longer than nine months. Even if Jean agrees.

Ronnie Can't you do it unilaterally? Say, on grounds of adultery?
David Yes, but the adulterer's meant to be the reluctant party.

Pause

Ronnie You don't think this is a good idea, do you?
David No, Ronnie, I don't. I've never thought it a good idea that you insist on sleeping with a goodly proportion of your students. But even relative to your past form, actually proposing to marry one seems a peculiarly bad idea.
Ronnie I was relying on you to understand.
David That was unwise. Why?

Ronnie thinks

Ronnie Well, no-one else will.
David Are you surprised? Jean is the best thing that ever happened to you. She's kind, she's caring, she's loyal ... in fact, she's far too good for you.
Ronnie When you meet Melissa you'll understand.
David Melissa is the student?
Ronnie Yes. But she's no ordinary student.
David You mean she's pregnant?
Ronnie Besides that. Not only is she beautiful, she is also exceptionally bright. Straight alphas in all her internal assessments. Actually, I feel rather a fraud marking them. (*Little pause*) I mean, she's far cleverer than I am. For example, unlike me, she really seems to have a genuine grasp of what deconstructionism actually is.
David I thought you lectured on that.
Ronnie I do. Never understood it though. I thought no-one did. But she seems to. We were talking about it the other night ... in bed.
David You want to marry someone who talks about deconstructionism in bed?
Ronnie (*not listening*) And my God is she incredible in that department! I tell you, David, the younger generation of women! Wow wee! Fasten your seat-belts! None of this lie back and think of England stuff. They take the bull by the horns. And they know what they want. Boy, does she know what she wants.
David I won't ask what that is.
Ronnie Everything. The whole works. On top. End to end. Upside down. Doggy-style——
David (*cutting in*) I get the point.

Pause

What about Jean?
Ronnie Jean? The complete opposite. Never takes the initiative.
David I meant, what about your marriage to her? And your responsibilities to the children.
Ronnie Yes, but what about my responsibilities to Melissa? (*Little pause*) And let's face it. She's a younger woman. I mean, we don't keep on driving the same old car.

David shakes his head in disbelief

David God knows what she sees in an old man like you.
Ronnie Ah, but men and women age differently. How did Chaucer put it? "Bet than old beef is the tender veal but bet is the pike than the pickerel."

There is a knock at the door

David (*calling*) Yes.

Margaret enters with a bag. She is in her mid-forties, modestly but not dowdily dressed, and plain

Margaret Oh... Hello, Ronnie.
Ronnie Margaret.
David You were saying, Ronnie?
Ronnie I've finished, actually.
Margaret (*to David*) I just wanted a book. It's the end of term collection.
David Yes. Sorry, I meant to return them.
Margaret It's all right.
David Which one do you want?
Margaret Hume's *Essays*.
David Ah yes. *Moral, Political and Literary*. My bedtime reading. (*He moves left*)
Margaret You can have an extension if you want.
David No. I won't be needing them.

David exits

Margaret How is he?
Ronnie David?
Margaret Yes. Is he OK?
Ronnie I think so. Why?
Margaret He doesn't seem upset? Or depressed?
Ronnie No. Why should he be?

Margaret Maybe he's covering up.
Ronnie Covering what up?
Margaret The book, of course.
Ronnie Oh no. I really can't believe David has formed an emotional attachment to Hume's *Essays*. Even if he does go to bed with them.
Margaret Not that book.
Ronnie Oh, you mean his book? Has it been panned? I tend not to read the philosophical journals.
Margaret Not his book, his ex-wife's book. Penelope Kite. You don't mean you haven't heard?
Ronnie Oh, Penny's written another novel, has she? Why should that bother David? She's written hundreds. Penny got the writing bug the moment she stopped teaching English Literature. Or was it the moment she left David...?
Margaret She hasn't written another novel. She's written an autobiography.
Ronnie Ah. I see.
Margaret Ronnie, for an expert, you're not very up on the literary scene. It's been reviewed in all the papers.
Ronnie Well, I've been rather...
Margaret One of the tabloids even serialised it.
Ronnie Really, which one?

Margaret thinks

Margaret I think it was the *Sunday Times*.

Ronnie looks confused

And this evening she's on the radio, if you please.
Ronnie Really?
Margaret I just hope he's been too busy to notice.

A little pause

Ronnie Anyway, she's been rude about him, has she?
Margaret Rude about him? Let's just say it's below the belt. In every sense.
Ronnie What fun! I look forward to it.
Margaret Ronnie, how can you say that?
Ronnie Oh, come on. We all enjoy a bit of juicy gossip. Unless it's about us, of course. (*He laughs*)
Margaret As a matter of fact...
Ronnie What?
Margaret Well, you do get the odd mention.

Ronnie What! What does she say?

Margaret I don't remember exactly, but something about what a notorious lech you are——

Ronnie What——

Margaret And what a disgrace it is to this university that you're still employed here.

Ronnie Why, the complete——

Margaret Oh yes. And she says the worst thing is, you're not even a good fuck.

Ronnie is shattered

Her words, not mine.

Ronnie So now David will know...

Margaret That you're no good in bed?

Ronnie No! About me and Penny.

Margaret Well ... she does base the judgement on personal experience. Says you're prone to PME ... whatever that is.

Ronnie God...

Margaret Oh, I wouldn't worry about it too much if I were you. I mean, about David finding out. You see, he's known for years.

Ronnie What?

Margaret Yes.

Ronnie But he never gave any indication...

Margaret Well, you know David.

Ronnie He never said anything...

Margaret Probably didn't want to embarrass you.

Ronnie Are you sure he knows?

Margaret Absolutely. It was me who told him.

Ronnie What?

Margaret I think he's coming back.

Ronnie Oh God. Look, tell him I had to rush off.

Ronnie exits

David returns with a book

Margaret Ronnie had to rush off.

David Oh. (*Little pause*) Listen, Margaret. It was an accident. I know you'll be angry but at least give me credit for owning up and admitting it. I didn't have to say anything. In all likelihood, if it wasn't for my honesty you would never have known.

Margaret David, what are you talking about?

David I've spilt coffee on Hume's *Essays*.

He gives her the book. She smiles

Margaret What an example you are to the students.
David They won't know it was me.
Margaret That's not the point.
David Perhaps not entirely. But surely it would be worse if they did know?
I mean— (*he breaks off*) Sorry.

She goes to put the book down

Margaret Anyway, what have you been doing with yourself? We haven't
been seeing much of you.
David No.
Margaret You don't come into the library like you used to.
David No. The book. You know.
Margaret The book?
David Yes. Finishing it. Getting it published. All that.
Margaret Oh... Yes, of course. (*She walks around the room*) What else?
Anything caught your interest lately?

David thinks

David No, I don't think so. How do you mean?
Margaret Oh. I don't know. News ... an article in the paper ... anything...
David No. Actually, I've stopped taking the papers. They're full of what
German philosophers used to call the *Zeitgeist*. You know, here today,
gone tomorrow stuff. Throwaway material. The perennial questions don't
get much of a look-in. Why, there hasn't been a nuclear war has there?

Margaret laughs

Margaret No.
David Well, that's a relief. The effect on Game Theory would be devastating.

Margaret looks puzzled

Margaret I'm not even going to pretend I understand that remark. But it's
nice to see you haven't lost your sense of humour.
David Why should I have done?

She stops

Margaret Something's wrong.

Pause

David Why do you say that?
Margaret Something's wrong… I know it is…

Pause

David What do you mean?
Margaret I know what it is. Plato! Where's Plato? He's normally all over me. (*She calls*) Plato!
David Actually… Plato's dead.
Margaret What?

David nods. Margaret is speechless. Pause

When?
David Yesterday.
Margaret Yesterday! Oh, how awful.

Pause

What happened?
David I had to have him put to sleep.
Margaret Oh … poor thing. (*She nods sympathetically*) What was wrong with him?
David (*after a pause*) Well… I think it was just the right time.
Margaret Yes. I suppose he was getting on a bit, wasn't he? How old was he? Twelve, thirteen——
David Ten.
Margaret Was he? Oh, well. Double figures. That's not a bad innings, is it? That's seventy in dog years… And we all have to go sometime.
David Yes.
Margaret Still, you must feel lonely without him.

Pause

Oh, dear. How I've let your mother down.
David My mother?
Margaret Yes.
David But she's——
Margaret Yes, I know she's dead. *I* arranged the funeral. But before she

died I promised her I'd look after you. Look after you! Your dog dies and I don't even know about it.

David That wasn't your fault.

Pause

Margaret You're wearing the jumper I made you.

David ...It's my favourite.

Margaret I'm glad. But you've got thinner. Are you sure you're eating properly?

David I'm fine.

Margaret I'd be happy to come and cook for you. You know that.

David Thank you.

Pause

Margaret Actually, I wondered if you might like to come to supper tomorrow?

David Ah...

Margaret To celebrate your fiftieth birthday. (*She smiles*) I keep a note of it in my diary.

David How thoughtful. But I'm sorry, I'm afraid I can't.

Margaret Oh well. I should have given you more notice. I don't suppose you could do tonight?

David No... I can't do tonight either.

Margaret What about the day after tomorrow?

David No...

Margaret When then?

David Actually, I'm not feeling very sociable at the moment.

Pause

Margaret David, what's wrong?

David What do you mean?

Margaret Between us.

David Nothing. We're friends.

Margaret That's what I mean.

Pause

Didn't that night mean anything to you? Or are you going to leave me on the shelf like an old unread book?

Pause

David Look, Margaret... what happened after the funeral was just... I don't know. I think I had an emotional reaction of some sort. Basically, it was a mistake.
Margaret ...A mistake.
David Yes. I'm sorry.

Pause

Margaret I suppose there isn't much more to say, is there?
David I suppose not.

Pause

Margaret I'm sorry about Plato. (*She goes to the door*) You know where I am if you need me. (*She opens the door*)
David Margaret!

She turns round quickly

You forgot the book.

She takes it

> *Joanna, a smartly-dressed woman in her late twenties, appears in the doorway*

Joanna Professor Freeman?
David Yes.
Joanna (*coming in*) At last. This place is a rabbit warren. (*She holds out her hand*) Joanna Smart. How do you do.

They shake hands

David Hello.

Joanna offers Margaret her hand

Joanna And you must be Mrs Freeman?

Margaret reluctantly shakes hands

Margaret No.
Joanna Oh, well. Worth a shot.

Margaret I'm the librarian.
Joanna The librarian? Really? That must be fascinating.

A short pause

I mean, as long as you like books. And I love books. In fact, do you know, sometimes I lie awake at night thinking, God, I wish I was a librarian.
Margaret Believe me. It's not as fascinating as it sounds.

Pause

David Well, Miss, um...
Joanna Smart.
David What can I do for you?
Joanna Actually, most urgently, you could direct me to the little girls' room.
David What?
Margaret The loo.
Joanna Exactly. I'm bursting.
David Use mine. It's through there and immediately on your left.
Joanna Professor, you've just saved my life.

Joanna goes out

Margaret Who the hell is she?
David No idea.
Margaret Joanna Smart. The name rings a bell.
David Not for me.
Margaret Well. I'm not waiting to find out. Little girls' room, indeed!

She goes to the door but hesitates again

Oh, since I'm not going to see you in the foreseeable future ... I'd better give you this now. (*She looks in her bag*) I've just finished it. I was going to wrap it up, but ... (*She takes out a hand-knitted woolly jumper, not dissimilar to the one he's wearing, and gives it to him*) I hope it fits.

David holds the jumper and looks at it. He doesn't know what to say

David ...You really shouldn't have bothered.

A little pause

Margaret Happy birthday.

Margaret exits

He puts the jumper aside

Joanna enters

Joanna That's better. Where's your friend?
David She had to go.
Joanna Gone back to the library, has she? I hope I didn't drive her away. (*She smiles. She goes over to the window and looks out*) Actually, I remember her. You see, I was an undergraduate here.
David Oh, really?
Joanna She caught me writing obscenities in *Paradise Lost.* Reported me to the Dean. Personally, I thought it was fair comment.
David Quite.
Joanna I'm not surprised she didn't recognize me. I used to be a punk.
David And you read English?
Joanna Yes. (*Pause*) I got a First.
David Well done.
Joanna Not really. My tutor was on the examining board.
David I'm sure he treated you like everyone else.
Joanna Not unless he was bonking everyone else.

Pause

David Miss Smart, what did you come to see me about?

She thinks

Joanna I'll be straight with you. In a nutshell, the book.
David The book?
Joanna Yes. I'm from the *Guardian.* I want to interview you about it.

David is stunned

I'm sorry to spring it on you like this. I would have phoned, but as I'm here today anyway I thought I'd——
David Hang on. Let's get this absolutely straight. You want to interview me?
Joanna Yes.
David About the book?
Joanna Yes.
David For an article in the *Guardian*?

Joanna You've got it.

David smiles

David Well well well. I've really hit the big time, haven't I?
Joanna I suppose you could put it like that. So you'll do it?
David Of course.
Joanna Great. (*She takes out a note pad*) Oh, you don't mind if I use a tape recorder, do you?
David No. Why should I?
Joanna No reason. It's just some people hate the things. (*She rummages in her bag*)
David So there are still quality papers, after all. You know, I must confess, until now I'd rather underestimated the modern press. I assumed it was all sleazy sensationalism.

She takes out the tape recorder

Joanna We like to cover all points of view. (*She opens her note pad and turns on the tape recorder*) Right. Now ... basically, what do you think of the book?
David What do *I* think of it?
Joanna Yes.
David Well...uh...you won't be surprised to hear... I, uh...

Joanna waits expectantly

   Well, to be honest ... I think it's pretty damn good.

Pause

Joanna I beg your pardon?
David Yes. I think it's good.
Joanna Good?
David Yes. Very good, actually.

Pause

Joanna That's remarkable.
David Is it?
Joanna I think so.
David Why?
Joanna Well, that you can be so objective.

David I didn't say I was being objective. Whatever that may mean. I can only
  give my opinion.

Joanna hesitates

Joanna I must say, Professor. You've rather thrown me.
David Have I?
Joanna Yes. Um... (*She puts her notebook aside*) Well ... what is it, exactly,
  that you like about it?
David Oh, the usual things one looks for in a book of this kind. It's balanced.
  Every viewpoint is considered. Everyone's given a good crack of the whip.
  But that's not to say the author's afraid to make judgements. On the
  contrary, the book comes down firmly on one side of the argument. Very
  firmly. In short, sound premises, sound predicates, it's closely argued, its
  reasoning supports its conclusions.
Joanna Yes... But how do you think *you* come out of it?
David Me?
Joanna Yes, you personally.
David Well ... personally, I must admit ...
Joanna Yes?
David I think it enhances my reputation.

Pause

Joanna Enhances your reputation?
David Yes. Of course, I recognize that my peers may judge differently.
  Though I doubt it.
Joanna Professor, you astonish me.
David Look, Miss Smart, if you didn't like the book, why don't you just
  say so.
Joanna Me? I loved it. I think it's one of the most honest and gritty pieces
  of writing I've read in years.

David considers this

David Honest and gritty, eh? Yes. I rather like that. Thank you very much.
Joanna Professor, I really don't see that you're in a position to thank me.
David What?
Joanna Now, come on. You're not really playing the game, are you? You
  agreed to do an interview with me but everything you say is sarcastic,
  ridiculous or downright dishonest.
David I don't know why you say that. I've said exactly what I think.

Pause

Joanna You're a cold fish, aren't you? I can see exactly what she means.
David She?
Joanna Yes, your wife. Or do you refuse to recognize her existence?
David As a matter fact I do. I'm not married.
Joanna All right. Your ex-wife. God, what a pedant you are. I can see why
she left you.
David Miss Smart. Could you please tell me what my ex-wife has got to do
with this interview?
Joanna What's she got to do with this interview?
David Yes, I can't see her relevance to *Matters of Life and Death*.
Joanna *Matters of Life and Death*?
David Yes. The name of the book. Sorry, I assumed you read books before
you interviewed their authors.

Pause. She smiles and begins to laugh

What's so funny?
Joanna I haven't come to interview you about any *Matters of Life and Death*.
David What?
Joanna I've come to talk about your ex-wife's autobiography. It's just come
out. (*She takes it out of her bag and passes it to him*) I can't believe you
didn't know.

Pause. He begins to read at the point where it was marked

Yes … well, of course, ideally I'd give you a chance to read the book before
you commented on it but unfortunately I haven't got much time. I've got
to hunt around for some more news. You know, date-rapes, student
suicides, tampon taxes, that sort of thing. So if we could make a fresh
start… (*She picks up her pad again and rewinds the tape*) I tell you what.
I'll make it easy for you. I won't ask you any questions that assume any
knowledge on your part. Of the book, that is. Not your marriage.

*The tape finishes rewinding. She presses the record button. She reads the
questions from her pad*

Penelope says that after the first year of your marriage you completely lost
interest in her sexually and showed more affection to your dog … a
relationship she doubts was purely platonic. I quote, "David and Plato were
so mutually adoring I wouldn't be surprised if they gave each other blow-
jobs". Any comment?

Pause

No. OK. How about... (*She looks through her pad*) Is it true that you intentionally tormented Penelope by remaining coldly indifferent to her blatant promiscuity?

Pause

All right. We'll play it your way. Suppose you just tell me, in your own words, why you think the marriage broke up?

Pause

Professor, I should warn you. If you remain silent, readers may draw their own conclusions. ...Have you nothing to say?

He hands her back the book

David Yes. I'd like you to go, please.
Joanna (*taking the book*) What?
David Leave. Please.
Joanna Listen, I came all the way from London to do this. And to be quite frank, I was hoping for something a bit more juicy than a critique of your dry-as-dust philosophical treatise, and not a word on your celebrated ex-wife's best-selling memoirs. I mean, considering you've just been immortalised as about the most unattractive man in England, one might reasonably expect that you'd jump at the chance to have your say. Unless, of course, you accept her version...

David puts the book and the tape recorder into her bag

What are you doing?

He takes her by the arm

Hey! Don't touch me! Don't you dare——

He escorts her to the door

Look, I'm warning you. You are assaulting me. Do you realize that? You are assaulting the Deputy Editor of the *Guardian* Women's Page. Get your hands off me. I can't believe this. You are actually assaulting me. She says you're a misogynist but I didn't know you were violent. You're going to be sorry for this. I'm going to kill you. I'm really going kill you. When this article comes out, you're gonna be dead!

Joanna exits

He shuts the door behind her. Pause. He breathes deeply. Shortly, there is a knock at the door

David (*opening the door*) Yes!

Tom enters

(*Quietly*) Oh… Hello, Tom.
Tom Is everything all right?
David All right? Yes. Fine, thanks.
Tom (*unconvinced*) Good.

Pause

That woman who just left, I'm sure I recognize her.
David She's a journalist. Her name's Joanna Smart.
Tom Joanna Smart. Of course. She was an undergraduate here, wasn't she?
David I believe so.
Tom Yes… So you keep in touch, do you?
David No.

Pause

Tom Yes. I remember her well. For some reason *Paradise Lost* springs to mind. And then, of course, there was that rather unfortunate business. You know. The usual thing. I tried to persuade her to keep it but … well… (*He reflects*)
David Tom, is there anything in particular you wanted to see me about?
Tom Yes … actually, it's about the book.

Pause

David My ex-wife's book?
Tom Yes. I didn't like to mention it when Ronnie was here… Anyway, I just wanted to tell you … the Senior Common Room wanted to tell you … that … well… we're all taking it with a pinch of salt. (*He smiles*) Just to put your mind at rest.

Pause

Are you really all right? I mean your life hasn't exactly been a bed of roses recently, has it? What with your mother dying ... and ... I mean, if I had an ex-wife who did something like that——

David Tom... I don't give a damn about Penelope's book. Or, indeed, Penelope. ...I was glad to be rid of her. As for her book, I refuse to discuss it further. I'm already utterly bored by the subject. ... But then most things bore me these days.

Tom looks puzzled

I'm sorry, that wasn't meant to be profound.

Tom Are you sure you're all right?

David Tom, I wish you'd stop asking me that.

Tom Well, it's just you do sound a little low.

David I'm fine. All right? I'm perfectly happy. I'm just a bit bored. That's all. Don't you ever feel that way? Don't you get bored of endless services? Or do you still feel a *frisson* every time you step up to the pulpit?

Tom Yes. I do, actually.

David Really...? I don't think many people retain the enthusiasm of youth at our age. One loses interest. Well, I have, anyway. (*He goes to the window*) Take this place, for example. I used to love it. Even after years of living here I would quite often find myself just gazing out of the window and thinking how beautiful it was. But now it leaves me cold. And it's the same with all the other things I used to love. Music ... good food ... books ... even philosophy. (*He smiles*) It's funny now to think of it, but you know Marx's line about how philosophers had described the world but the point is to change it? Well, that was my ambition. Through the power of my imagination and intellectual rigour I was going to change the world!

Pause

But now... I'm just bored. Bored of everything. It's a philosophical position I've arrived at, really. I even thought of writing a book about it.

Tom Why didn't you?

David Couldn't be bothered.

Pause

Right now I can't think why I bothered to finish the last one. Hardly anyone will bother to read it. (*He picks up a copy of his book*) It's rather embarrassing, but just now, that journalist, Joanna Smart, she said she wanted to talk about a book. Of course, as you did, she meant Penelope's book. But for a moment—more than a moment, actually—I thought she meant my book. And I thought, perhaps, in the future, you know...

Tom nods. David smiles and puts the book down

Oh, what's it matter.

Tom David——

David Did you know that Russian Roulette was invented by White Russian soldiers not as a torture or anything, but simply as a game to relieve boredom? And when Graham Greene was at Oxford, he was so bored that he played it too. He played it six times, which means his chance of surviving was five sixths to the power of six, which comes out as fractionally more than one in three. So old Graham was pretty lucky ... or unlucky... I suppose if one didn't know where one's next meal was coming from one wouldn't have time to be -

He sees Tom looking at his watch

I'm sorry, Tom. Am I boring you?

Tom No, David. I think we should talk more about this. (*He pauses*) And I wish it could be now... (*He gets up*) But unfortunately I must go. I'm having lunch with the Dean.

David Then of course you must go.

Tom hesitates

Tom We'll talk again later.

Tom exits

David goes to the door and locks it. He draws the curtains. The only remaining source of light is the desk lamp. He goes over to the desk. He sits. He puts the photograph face down again. Pause. He opens the drawer and takes out the sleeping pills, the plastic bag and the elastic band. He empties the pills on to the desk. Pause. He takes the phone off the hook. Then he reaches over behind the desk and unplugs the phone. He picks up two pills and swallows them. He repeats this process several times. When he's finished, he brings the plastic bag down over his head. He breathes deeply inflating and deflating the plastic bag. Then he lets his hands fall and the plastic bag is sealed against his neck. Shortly, his head slumps on to the desk

Pause

Bob's whistling is heard as he comes up from the cellar. Shortly, he enters with his tool box. As he speaks, he puts his tool box down on the nearest surface, opens it, rummages inside, takes out a cloth and wipes his hands before closing the tool box again and taking it to the door

Bob Are you allergic to daylight, Professor, or what? ...Anyway, I'm off to eat me sandwiches. Wouldn't mind washing them down with a drop of that Beaujolais. You've got enough booze down there to last you a lifetime... Oh, just to be on the safe side, don't touch the light switch. The damp's got into it and I've had to disconnect the earth to do the rewiring. Right, I'll be back this afternoon to finish you off. (*He goes to the door but then stops*) Oh, I'll need to be let in. You're not going anywhere, are you? (*He looks up*) Professor...? (*He moves towards David and sees the plastic bag. He drops the tool box*)

Suddenly, the last frenetic sequence of "Winter" from The Four Seasons *plays. During this, Bob rushes over to David. He rips off the plastic bag and the elastic band. He holds David's head up, puts his ear to David's mouth and listens. He sees the empty pill bottle on the desk. He picks it up and reads the label. He picks up the phone and dials but can't get a dialling tone. He rushes to the door, tries to open it, but finds it locked*

He unlocks it and runs out

A shaft of light comes in through the open door

Fade to Black-out

The music ends

ACT II

The same

The sound of rain falling. The Lights come up

The room is empty. The curtains are open but it is dark. The door is shut, the photograph is standing up again and the phone is back on the hook. The rain slowly dies away

Pause. The phone rings. It rings a few times. It stops. We hear David's recorded message from the answering machine: "Hello. This is David Freeman. I'm afraid I'm out at the moment but if you wait for the tone you can leave a message and I'll call you back later."

The tone

Ronnie (*on the line*) Hi, David. It's me again. Ronnie. Ring me, will you? I'm in need of a bit of a chat.

Pause

Where are you anyway? You never go out. In fact ... I bet you're there, aren't you? You're there working but not answering the phone. Like you were this morning. Well, please stop and pick it up *now*.

Pause

You're not. OK. Sorry about that. But, look, there's no-one else I can talk to about this so I'll just talk, if you don't mind. (*Pause*) Something terrible's happened. She ... um, actually, if anyone's with you when you listen to this, stop the tape. OK? I'll give you a few seconds.

The door opens and Tom enters in his cassock. He reaches for the light switch by the door. The Light flickers but doesn't come on. He turns the switch off and on again. Still no light

Right.

Tom starts

Tom Hello?
Ronnie Ready?
Tom What?
Ronnie It's Melissa.

Tom is confused

She doesn't want to marry me.

Tom succeeds in turning the Light on and realizes the voice is coming from the answerphone. As Ronnie talks, Tom draws the curtains and listens

I hadn't anticipated that. I mean, she said she wanted to the other night...
Anyway, then we had a terrible row. About the baby, of course. She still
seems determined to have it. So I rather lost my temper I'm afraid. And said
a few things I regret. But I do think with some justification. After all, if she
drops that sprog, she's not only ruining her life, she's also ruining mine.
I mean, if the Dean were to find out ... young people are so selfish. But all
is not yet lost. I'm taking her out to dinner at a rather romantic little
Lebanese place——

Tom picks up the phone

David?
Tom This is the Chaplain speaking.

Silence

Are you still there?

A little pause

Ronnie No.
Tom What? ...Ronnie? Ronnie?

*We hear the dialling tone. Tom puts the phone down. He thinks for a moment.
Then he picks up the phone and starts dialling*

Margaret enters

*He stops dialling and puts the phone down. They look at each other for a
moment. Then she embraces him*

There, there...

She keeps hold of him

Margaret I'm sorry.
Tom Don't be silly.

She pulls away

Margaret Thank you.

Pause

He's not here yet?
Tom No. (*He closes the door*)
Margaret (*after a pause*) Tom. There's something I need to tell you before he gets back. After his mother's funeral I came back here with David and ... something happened ... that shouldn't have happened... And then something that should have happened, didn't happen ... and now it hasn't happened again. (*Pause*) Do you see what I mean?

Tom thinks

Tom You're pregnant?
Margaret I think so.
Tom I don't believe it. (*Pause*) When will you know for sure?
Margaret Any time I choose.
Tom What?
Margaret Yesterday I bought a do-it-yourself test from the chemist. All it needs is a urine sample and it tells you in three minutes. (*Pause*) But I haven't had the guts to take it.
Tom In case it's positive?
Margaret In case it's not.
Tom (*surprised*) You mean you want...
Margaret Time's running out for me...

Tom thinks

Tom Where is this test?
Margaret In my bag.
Tom You could take it now.
Margaret Now? (*She thinks*) But what if David came back?
Tom You have to tell him sometime. (*Little pause*) And it might make him

change his mind. (*Pause*) The hospital fear he may try again. They wanted him to stay longer but he discharged himself. As he's not insane, there wasn't much they could do.

Margaret thinks. Then she picks up her bag and takes it off

Pause. Tom picks up the phone and dials

Oh, hello. Could I speak to the Dean, please? ... Thank you. (*He waits*) John. Tom here. Sorry to bother you but something rather important's come up. ... No, actually, this has got nothing to do with David—he's not back from the hospital yet. It concerns Ronald Drake. ... Actually, I'd rather speak to you in person, if possible. It's rather delicate...

Margaret enters

Yes, after Evensong is fine. ... Right. Bye. (*He replaces the receiver*)

A pregnant pause

Margaret (*quietly*) I couldn't go.

Tom is puzzled

I mean, I tried but... (*She shrugs*) I don't know. I think it's this place. And with David about to come back... Anyway, I think I'd better go.
Tom Go?
Margaret Away from here. I'll come back when I know.

Margaret exits

Tom sits on the sofa, puts his hands together and waits. Pause. He looks at his watch. He gets up and switches on the stereo. He tunes the radio and listens. A woman interviewer is laughing

Interviewer (*on the radio*) Oh, how wonderful!
Penelope (*on the radio*) Yes, it was a very happy childhood.
Interviewer If you've just joined us, I'm talking to the novelist, Penelope Kite, about her newly published autobiography, *Good Times Bad Times*. Now Penny, on a more serious note, the person in your life who comes in for, perhaps, the most criticism is your first husband, the philosopher David Freeman.
Penelope Yes, that was definitely one of the bad times. He was, of course, very ... intellectually stimulating, but, well, shall we say, personal warmth wasn't his strong point. ...Except towards his mother.

Tom notices the plastic bag on the floor. He goes to it, picks it up and examines it

Unnoticed by Tom, David enters, looking wet and bedraggled. He sees Tom and hesitates

During the following, Tom puts the plastic bag in the bin. He takes it out again and tears it before putting it back in the bin

Interviewer Can I ask you, have you spoken to him since the book's publication?
Penelope No. We haven't been in contact for years.
Interviewer Do you think he'll be hurt by what you've written?

Tom turns his attention to the desk. He picks up a paper-knife and tests its point. He then tries a drawer and pulls out Final Exit. *He considers throwing it in the bin but then decides against it and puts it back in the drawer*

Penelope No. Not particularly. He's fairly thick-skinned. Anyway, most likely, he'll never read it. Up there in his ivory tower he's pretty much dead to the world. And he has few, if any, friends. You see, the thing about David is that he cares very little for other people. He has no need of them. All he really wants to do is to get on with his work. His *Weltanschauung*, as he would call it, is essentially anti-social. Whereas I, of course, love people. Hence, the disaster that was our marriage.

Tom tries another desk drawer but finds it locked. David goes to the stereo

Interviewer Your second marriage has been much happier.
Penelope Immeasurably——

David switches off the radio. Tom turns round. An awkward pause

Tom You're soaking.
David Yes. I seem to have gone out without my coat. (*Pause*) Tom, what exactly are you doing here?
Tom David ... I just want you to know ... the Senior Common Room want you to know ... that we're all praying for you.
David ...So everyone knows?
Tom Well ... the hospital phoned.

David nods

I hear they had to...

David Pump my stomach out?

Tom Yes. How do you feel?

David Angry.

Tom I meant physically.

David I know you did. Pretty lousy, thanks. (*Little pause*) Right. Well, thank you for being here to welcome me back. I appreciate your concern.

Tom It was the least I could do.

David And I'm sure you've lots of other things to do.

Tom Yes...

David Well, then. There's really no need for you to stay any longer.

Tom Oh, that's all right. I'm quite happy to keep you company for a bit. Shall I make some tea?

David thinks

David Ah, Tom, no. I don't think you quite understand. What I'm trying to say is that I'd actually *prefer* to be alone.

Tom No, David, I understand. I'd just prefer you not to be.

Pause

David Why?

Tom I think you know why.

David Tom, if I wanted to try again immediately, instead of taking the bus home I would have thrown myself under it.

Tom I'm sorry, David, but I insist that for tonight, at least, someone is here to look after you.

Pause

David Right, well, since you seem to be staying, for the moment... (*he closes the door*) perhaps I will have that tea.

Tom Certainly.

David (*relieving Tom of the paper-knife*) Thank you.

Tom hesitates before going off R

David immediately goes to the desk and tries a drawer. Finding it locked, he goes to the bookcase and takes out a book. He takes a key from the space left by the book, replaces the book and unlocks the drawer. He opens it, reaches to the back and takes out a revolver. He fondles it for a moment and thinks. Pause. He replaces the revolver, locks the drawer and puts the key back in his pocket. He goes towards the passage L

Simultaneously, Tom enters R *with a tray, on which are cups and saucers, sugar and milk*

Tom Where are you going?

David turns round

David To change my clothes. If that's all right with you?

A knock at the door

Get that for me, will you?

David exits L

Tom answers the door

It's Laura. She is dressed for an evening out

Laura Oh. I was expecting Professor Freeman.
Tom Yes... Is he expecting you?
Laura Well ... not exactly.
Tom Actually, David's been taken ill.
Laura Oh. I'm sorry to hear that. Nothing serious, I hope?
Tom I'm afraid it was. He had to go to hospital.
Laura No!
Tom I'm afraid so. And he's still not feeling well. So I think, perhaps, it would be best...
Laura Of course. I won't disturb him. (*She hesitates*)
Tom I could take a message?
Laura Oh, it's nothing important. Just say, Laura stopped by.

David enters wearing a dressing gown over his trousers, and slippers. He dries his hair with a towel

David (*brightly*) Ah, my American friend!
Laura Professor!
David Do come in.
Laura Oh, but I don't want to disturb you.
David You won't. Come and join our little tea party.
Laura Well ... thank you.
David The Chaplain's playing mother.

Laura comes in. Tom shuts the door

Tom Would you like some tea?

Laura No, thank you. Professor, I'm sorry to hear you're sick.

David Sick? (*He looks at Tom and smiles*) So that's what he's been telling you, is it? You fibber.

Laura But you went to the hospital?

David Oh yes, I went to hospital. Or rather, I was taken to hospital. But I'm not sick. Unless, of course, to be suicidal is *ex hypothesi* to be sick.

Laura What?

David By the way, how was the symposium? Organ transplants, wasn't it? (*To Tom*) She gave a paper on kidneys. Could have had mine by now if everything had gone smoothly.

Tom David...

David Yes, Tom?

Tom This isn't fair on her.

Laura (*recovering her composure*) Actually, it's all right. I do counselling at Berkeley.

David Do you? Oh, well. I expect you're going to start counselling me then, are you?

Laura Not if you don't want me to.

David Well, as a matter of fact, I don't. It so happens I've had just about enough people interfering in my life for one day. Or, more precisely, my death. Doctors, electricians and now chaplains.

The phone rings. Tom is about to answer it but David pre-empts him

Excuse me. (*He picks up the phone*) Hello? (*He listens for a moment*) This is David Freeman. I'm afraid I'm *in* at the moment but if you wait till I'm *out* you can call back later and leave a message. (*He replaces the receiver*) A journalist... Why can't people accept that if someone wants to kill himself he should bloody well be left alone to do it? I mean, who do they think they are? God...? Oh, sorry, Tom. (*Little pause*) Actually, I'm not sorry. Why should I be sorry? Look, Tom, I've known you for years but I've never said this to you before. Don't know why not. Didn't want to offend you or something. But now I'm going to. All right?

Pause

I don't believe in God. ... Actually, to say that I don't believe in God puts my belief in God too high. I have no coherent conception of the concept of God. I mean, what is he—or she—or it—or them? Some bearded little man sitting in the sky? Or some kind of amorphous ... thingummyjig? Either way, I think it's a load of hogwash. Which means, I conclude, that your whole life has been a complete waste of time.

An awkward pause

Tom I'll get the tea.

Tom goes out

Pause

Laura I better go. There's a symposium dinner. Actually, that's why I stopped by. I was going to invite you to come along, but...
David No, thank you.

Laura leaves reluctantly

Tom enters with a pot of tea. He goes to the tray and begins pouring the tea

Sorry. All I meant was don't try a last-minute conversion.
Tom You make it sound like a rugby match. Anyway, I wasn't going to.
David Good.

Tom gives David his tea and takes his own to the sofa. He sits down

Tom The answer is to find your own way to God.
David ...Tom, how can I find the answer when I don't understand the question? (*Little pause*) And I'm not a great one for belief, even when I do understand what I'm meant to be believing. ... What I value is knowledge.
Tom But if one's belief is true ... then it is knowledge.
David Ah, but is it? (*Pause*) A man is walking in the countryside when he sees a dog in a field. At least he thinks it's a dog. In fact, it's a sheep. But behind the sheep, there is a dog. Question: Does he *know* there's a dog in the field?

Tom is puzzled

The answer is, it depends on whether knowledge is true belief or justified true belief. I think it's justified true belief. And since that's what I value, I'm not going to believe there's a dog out there until I can really see it.

Pause

Tom Tolstoy was suicidal at your age—some kind of mid-life crisis—but he found faith and lived till he was eighty-two.

David ...OK, Tom. I'll make this hard for myself. Say, for the sake of
argument, that I'm a Christian. Why shouldn't I kill myself?

Tom Because life is sacred. It is a gift from God.

David More like a loan, wouldn't you say?

Tom It is for God to determine when we die. Taking life is to interfere in
God's decisions.

David Saving life is just as interfering and you don't think that's wrong.

Tom That's different.

David Why?

Tom Taking life is ... a waste.

David considers this

David Unless God takes it?

Pause

Tom There are plenty of secular reasons for you to stay alive too.

David Like what?

Tom Well ... how about the undergraduates?

David How do you mean?

Tom Well, it wouldn't set a very good example, would it? They look to their
Professor of Ethics for moral guidance.

David You fear a spate of copycat killings?

Pause

Tom David, I have no wish to engage in an intellectual sparring match. Let's
just talk plainly. This morning you were telling me that you were bored
with life. You'd lost your enthusiasm. Well, that's only natural. In later life
one does not have the advantages of youth.

David Exactly. That's why later life doesn't interest me.

Tom Ah, but there can be compensatory advantages. Have you considered,
for example, the possibility of, perhaps, marrying, and starting a family?

David laughs

What's so funny? That's what most people do.

David I've tried marriage. And as for procreation ... isn't it just an animal
instinct to reproduce our genes—a mindless lunge at immortality?

Tom Many people believe having children gives meaning to their lives.

David True. But is that belief justified? If life has no meaning, what good
is there in multiplying? How can life be given meaning by creating more

lives? …Anyway, thank God I didn't impregnate Penelope. Think what her children would be like.

Pause. Tom looks at his watch

Tom Margaret ought to be here.

David considers this

David Ought she…?
Tom I'm late for Evensong.
David In what sense?
Tom What?
David When you said "ought", did you mean it in the simply predictive sense that you expected her to be here, or in a moral sense, for example, in fulfilment of her obligations of friendship? Say, to stop me killing myself?
Tom Both.
David …I see. You've set up some kind of rota system, have you?
Tom David, given your intimacy, I think you at least owe her an explanation.

David is surprised

I understand the obligations go beyond friendship. So you really ought to talk to her. In the moral sense.

A little pause

David Very well. I'll talk to her. I'll try and explain. But it won't do any good.
Tom …You may be surprised.

There is a knock at the door

That must be her.

Tom goes to answer the door. David turns away. Tom opens the door

It's Joanna. She is put out for a moment but then sees David and puts her finger to her lips

Tom looks at his watch and exits

Joanna (*coming in*) Surprise!

David turns round

Professor, I've come to apologise. This morning I marched in without warning, failed to explain properly the purpose of my visit and then proceeded to interrogate you about your private life in the most impertinent fashion. I quite understand your refusal to speak to me on the phone. But I just want you to know, I'm sorry. (*She brings out a bunch of flowers from behind her back*) Very sorry. Very sorry indeed. Naturally, I've held back the article. I shoved in a stand-by piece instead. ... *Vaginal orgasms: Myth or Reality?*
David What do you want?
Joanna Well, personally I'm happy with the clitoral kind.

David shakes his head

Oh, I see what you mean. With you? Just an interview. (*She moves left with the flowers*) Shall I put these in water? They'll die otherwise.
David Just leave them there. (*He indicates the drinks table*)

She puts the flowers down on it

Miss Smart, I accept your apology but I thought I made it abundantly clear that I have no intention of discussing my ex-wife's memoirs.
Joanna Nor do I. I'm talking about your suicide attempt.

David is surprised

Which is not to say the two aren't linked. That's one of the things I'd like to find out. Seeing as my visit this morning was obviously the catalyst, I think it's my journalistic, not to say moral, duty to delve a little deeper. So... (*She takes out her tape recorder and switches it on*) Have you attempted suicide before?
David Hang on——
Joanna I mean it can't just have been because of the book? That was the last straw, was it?
David How do you know about this?
Joanna I'm afraid I can't tell you that. I have to protect my sources. (*Sympathetically*) When did you first become depressed?
David I'm not depressed.
Joanna Is there a history of depression in your family?
David Look, I'm not depressed. I just want to kill myself. There's a difference.
Joanna Or perhaps you feel unfulfilled in some way?
David Why should I talk to you about this?
Joanna Professor Freeman, since I'm going to write about you anyway, wouldn't you rather it was accurate?

Pause

David As a matter of fact, I feel completely fulfilled.
Joanna Why?
David Because my work is complete.

Joanna thinks

Joanna Your work? I see. It's a publicity stunt.
David What?
Joanna Feeling overshadowed by your wife's success, you hoped, by committing suicide, to win some attention for your own work. Albeit posthumously.
David Don't be ridiculous.
Joanna Why? You wouldn't be the first. And you must feel overshadowed? Her sales figures will inevitably outstrip yours.
David I don't regard sales figures as the measure of success.
Joanna Or is it revenge? By committing suicide after the publication of her book you make her responsible, both in her own eyes and the eyes of others.
David This has nothing to do with my ex-wife or her book.
Joanna So what do I tell my readers?
David I'm sure you can invent something.

A little pause

Joanna Not ideal. (*She thinks*) You're terminally ill?
David No.
Joanna HIV positive?
David ...No.
Joanna You're not a Lloyd's Name, are you?
David Fortunately, as a poor academic, I've never been rich enough to incur unlimited liability.
Joanna You're being pursued by the Child Support Agency?
David Surely you know Penelope didn't want children. Her novels were to be her children.
Joanna But since Penelope?
David The question hasn't arisen.

She thinks

Joanna I'll be honest with you. I'm running out of ideas.

He picks up the tape recorder

David Why don't you just tell your readers this. (*Into the tape recorder*) The only thing we have to look forward to in life is death. And the more so as we get older. What else does old age have in store for us? Realistically, one can expect both physical and mental decline, increased dependence on others, lower self-esteem ... in a word, decay. Better to quit while the going's good. You see, I share Nietzsche's view that few people die too early and most die too late. The trick is to die at the right time. (*He puts the tape recorder down again*)

Joanna Tell me about your childhood.

David My childhood has nothing to do with anything.

Joanna Oh, come, Professor. For all its limitations, surely psychoanalysis has taught us something.

David My problems began with my marriage.

Joanna OK. Tell me about your marriage.

David Now, listen——

Joanna OK. We'll go back to your childhood. Your ex-wife says your father died in the war. Is that correct?

David Yes. He was killed at Arnhem.

Joanna Before you were born?

David Yes.

Joanna Any brothers or sisters?

David No.

A short pause

Joanna I see. A posthumous only child. Doesn't look good, does it? What about your relationship with your mother?

David My mother and I were very close.

Joanna Were?

David She died two months ago.

Joanna Ah. And you're finding it difficult to come to terms with?

David On the contrary, it was a great release. She'd had cancer for some time. She wanted to die.

Joanna (*indicating*) Is that her in the photograph?

David Yes.

She nods approvingly

Joanna She looks strong. (*Abruptly*) So you have no living relatives?

David Actually, I have a second cousin in Australia. I've never met her and she may not even know of my existence. But she soon will. She's the sole beneficiary under my will. Not that I have much to leave her. (*A thought strikes him*) I do have one rather nice memento, though. It was my father's. Would you like to see it?

Joanna I'd love to.

David unlocks the drawer and pulls out the revolver. Joanna starts

David This would enliven your story, wouldn't it? Perhaps you'd like to take photographs. Before... (*he presses the nozzle to his temple*) and after.
Joanna Is that thing loaded?
David I'll just check.

He pulls the trigger. It clicks

No.
Joanna You knew it wasn't, didn't you?

He smiles

David Well, Miss Smart, it's been a fascinating trip down Memory Lane——
Joanna Are you going to try again?
David (*after a pause*) What do you think?
Joanna I don't think you tried the first time. Not really. A melodramatic gesture, that's all. Like with the gun. After all, you must have realized that electrician would find you. A classic cry for help.
David God help me...
Joanna All right then. You were serious. But if you are going to try again ... how? Are you going for the sleeping pills and plastic bag again?
David No more sleeping pills.
Joanna How then?

A short pause

The gun? (*She looks at him*) No. You obviously don't have any bullets.
David How did you find out about the first attempt?

She thinks

Joanna I was at the hospital when they brought you in. Collecting statistics on student pregnancies, student abortions, student suicides. You were a sort of bonus. (*Pause*) Actually, it was rather moving. I held your hand.
David You held my hand?
Joanna Yes.
David Why?
Joanna Well, I had to look the part, didn't I? I told them I was your wife.

Pause

David Miss Smart, I'm now going to wash my hands. Feel free to let yourself out. (*He makes to leave*)
Joanna But you haven't told me how yet. Or when?

He smiles

David Let's just say, I have no intention of reaching fifty. Keep the flowers.

David goes off

Joanna puts the tape recorder in her bag

Ronnie enters hesitantly. He wears a jacket and tie

Ronnie Well I be damned! If it isn't ... (*He thinks*)
Joanna You don't even remember my name.
Ronnie Of course, I do. It's ... it's ... on the tip of my tongue.
Joanna Joanna.
Ronnie Joanna. Of course. Joanna ... Sharp. That's it. You're a journalist now, aren't you? What are you doing here?
Joanna You broke my hymen but you can't even remember my name. I'm Smart. Not Sharp.

Pause

Ronnie Sorry.

Pause

   Look, how about I make it up to you? Over dinner.
Joanna I have to get back to London.
Ronnie Why? You can stay the night with me. (*He smiles seductively*) For old time's sake? As it happens, I've already booked a table.
Joanna As it happens, I've got an appointment with my Editor.
Ronnie For tomorrow's edition?
Joanna For dinner.

Pause

Ronnie I see. You're in a relationship?
Joanna You could say that.
Ronnie Is he married?

She hesitates

Joanna Yes.
Ronnie He's a fool. He should stick with his wife.
Joanna I agree. I am his wife. (*She puts on her coat*)

Pause

By the way … seeing as you're here and I'm here…
Ronnie (*eagerly*) Yes?
Joanna I mean, I don't want you to think I planned this…
Ronnie I won't.
Joanna …because it really doesn't mean that much to me.
Ronnie I understand.
Joanna Well, I might as well tell you. In my third year—just before Finals…
I got pregnant.

Ronnie is stunned

Ronnie Not you too?
Joanna What?
Ronnie I mean… (*He stares at the ground like a naughty schoolboy*) Sorry.

Joanna picks her bag up. A thought strikes him and he looks up

My God! You didn't keep it, did you?

*Pause. Joanna puts down her bag. She walks up to him, puts her hands on
his shoulders and leans towards him. Their eyes meet and they smile. She
knees him in the balls. He gasps, grabs them and doubles up in pain*

Joanna picks up her bag and leaves

Still sore, Ronnie undoes his trousers, puts his hands down them and rubs

Shortly, David enters and watches him

David You've got a problem.
Ronnie What?
David You can't keep it still for one moment, can you? I mean you have both
a wife and a fiancée and yet you still——
Ronnie She kneed me in the balls.
David Ah. What did you do to deserve that?
Ronnie I didn't deserve it. It was for something that happened years ago.

God, why do women have to get pregnant? (*He rubs himself*) Anyway, I won't be making any more babies.

David Well, that's something.

Ronnie And I haven't got a wife and a fiancée. Don't you listen to your answerphone messages? Other people do.

David What?

Ronnie The Chaplain for one. What was he doing here? And where have you been? I've been trying to get hold of you all afternoon.

Pause

David You don't know?

Ronnie Know what? (*Pause*) What have you been up to? This morning I find you in suspiciously close contact with an American you claim you've never met before and now you're in your dressing gown with my former lover.

Pause

David Have you seen Margaret?

Ronnie (*surprised*) No. Why?

David Never mind. So what you have you been up to?

Ronnie I've been with Melissa trying to persuade her to marry me. But she won't.

David Why not?

Ronnie She says I'm too selfish, too old and I'm doing it for the wrong reasons.

David Sounds like a bright girl.

Ronnie And, anyway, Catholics don't recognize divorce.

David Ah ... of course. Oh, well. I'm sure it's for the best. Now you can stick with Jean.

Ronnie No, I can't.

David Why not?

Ronnie Because I told her I wanted a divorce.

David Why did you do that?

Ronnie So that I could marry Melissa.

David I see. Counting your chickens.

Ronnie Yes...

Pause

David Well, since you're now not going to marry Melissa, why don't you go and tell Jean that you don't want a divorce?

Ronnie I have.
David What did she say?
Ronnie She wants a divorce.

Pause

That's not all. Melissa was supposed to meet me at a Lebanese restaurant. But she didn't turn up.
David Really Ronnie, I'd have thought a broken dinner date was the least of your problems.
Ronnie She was with the Dean. He sent for her.
David Why?
Ronnie Tom heard me on your bloody answerphone...
David Ah. So the Dean knows about you.
Ronnie Yes.
David And the baby?
Ronnie Yes.
David I see.
Ronnie No, you don't. It gets worse. She also said that *I* said that if she didn't have an abortion I would fail her internal assessment. I mean, can you beat it?
David It isn't true?
Ronnie Well, of course it isn't. What kind of person do you think I am?
David I'd better not answer that. She's a liar then?
Ronnie Yes. (*Little pause*) Well, not exactly a liar. I mean, I may, in the heat of the moment, have made some idle remark—but the point is, can you believe she took it seriously?

Pause

David You know, Ronnie, the thing about you is that you have absolutely no self-knowledge. Except, perhaps, of the carnal variety.
Ronnie What? Look, please, David. Rally round. I have an appointment with the Dean in five minutes. (*Little pause*) Come with me. I need your support.

Pause

David No, Ronnie.
Ronnie What?
David In the first place, it wouldn't do you any good, and, in the second place, I wouldn't even if it would.
Ronnie (*getting desperate*) David, you don't seem to understand. I'm going to lose my job.
David I'm sorry.

Ronnie is open-mouthed

Ronnie Oh God… (*He bursts into tears*)
David Ronnie… Ronnie… come on, old man … it's not as bad as all that…
Look, come and sit down. (*He leads Ronnie to the sofa and sits him down*)
Here. (*He gives him a handkerchief*) How about a drink?

*Ronnie nods. David fetches the bottle of whisky and is about to fill Ronnie's
glass. Instead, Ronnie takes the bottle and swigs from it*

There. (*Pause*) Now, look on the bright side. After all, the truth is they
should have got rid of you years ago.
Ronnie What the bloody——
David Oh, come on, Ronnie. You know it's true.

Ronnie goes quiet. Pause

Ronnie I should have taken that job in television. Years ago. I'd be
presenting *The South Bank Show* by now.

David smiles

David Listen, Ronnie. I have something to tell you. Everyone else knows so
it seems only fair that you should too. And after all our years together…
Anyway, I've decided to kill myself.

Ronnie is speechless

Actually, I'd be dead already but for a slight cock-up with the electrician.
Right. Now, you'd better run along or you'll be late for the Dean.
Ronnie You're not serious?
David I am.

Pause

Ronnie I can't believe it… Why?
David The usual reasons. You know, life being no longer worth living …
that sort of thing.
Ronnie I can't believe it…
David I expect it will sink in eventually.
Ronnie But … but …
David Please Ronnie, don't feel obliged to try and talk me out of it. There's
really no need. I've considered everything.
Ronnie David, you cannot kill yourself.

David sighs

…You just can't.
David Can't? Now that's a little unfair. Whatever carelessness I may have
shown, to fail to kill oneself once may still be regarded as a misfortune.
Ronnie Look, I know life gets tough. God knows, there have been times
when I've felt like ending it all. Like now actually. But one must go on.
David Really? Why?

Ronnie thinks

Ronnie One just must. People just do.
David Some don't.
Ronnie Most do.
David True. But most doing doesn't entail that I should, or even that most
should. The naturalistic fallacy. You can't derive an ought from an is.
You'll have to do better than that.
Ronnie Look, how would you feel if I threatened to kill myself?
David I see. The old role-reversal gambit. Ethics as empathy. But I'm afraid
it cuts little ice with me. I'm a professional, you know. Besides, you'd
never kill yourself.
Ronnie Oh, wouldn't I?
David No.

Pause

Ronnie No, you're right actually. I wouldn't have the guts. But then what's
so gutsy about chickening out of life?
David Ah, the Aristotelian thrust. I thought you might try that one. Attack
my character and virtue. Suicide can be a cowardly choice. But not in my
case. In my case it's rational. I'm tired of life, so I'm choosing death.
Ronnie My God. What would happen if everyone did that?
David Now you're getting sophisticated. Kant's categorical imperative.
First formulation. Always act in such a way that you can will that your
maxim should become a universal law, commonly known as "what if
everyone did that?" A complete *a priori* guide to moral conduct. Needless
to say, in practice, completely useless. If everyone in the world tried to
come into this room we'd all be squashed to death. But that's no reason why
you and I shouldn't be here. Similarly, as my suicide is most unlikely to
have any global domino effect, your question is … irrelevant. So, don't get
moral with me, Ronnie. It doesn't suit you.

Pause

Ronnie All right. So you have all the answers. But I do think it would be tragic.

David considers this

David Tragic?
Ronnie Yes.
David In what sense? Do you see me as a tragic hero with a single flaw or did you mean tragic in the merely colloquial sense?
Ronnie In the sense of it being a terrible waste. And a cause of great sadness to your friends.

Pause

David (*withoutflippancy*) I grant that my death will cause some sadness. One or two people will miss me a little ... at first. You ... Tom ... Margaret ... But that would be the same if I were going to live in Australia, or New Zealand, or anywhere you wouldn't see me again, and I'm sure you wouldn't kick up such a fuss about that. (*Pause*) However, in case anyone fails to see it that way, I did take the precaution of buying and posting several copies of *Suicide: A Guide for Those Left Behind*. I addressed one of them to you.
Ronnie Thanks. (*Pause*) Look. Just give it a bit more time. A year, a month, a week. Whatever. Time to cool off, to think again, to see how you feel——
David To recover my *joie de vivre*?
Ronnie Yes.
David My *raison d'être*?
Ronnie Exactly.
David I see. Having failed with the moral arguments, you now appeal simply to my prudence and self-interest. But it's no good, Ronnie. I've considered it from every angle. And I've had plenty of time to think about it.
Ronnie Yes. I think you think too much. (*Pause*) Isn't there anything I can do to stop you?
David Not within the realm of persuasion. And I trust you won't resort to coercion.
Ronnie (*not listening*) I saw a film once where a man sublimates his suicidal impulse by writing a play about it. You could write a play. Or a novel?
David Ronnie, I have no need of fictional escape.
Ronnie No. You're taking the direct route.
David No, it isn't an escape at all. That's a morally loaded description.
Ronnie What is it then?
David An exit. Just an exit. Perfectly timed. On cue. And avoiding what would otherwise be an anti-climax. (*Little pause*) Anyway, I've already

written about suicide. In the last chapter of my book. But not to sublimate it. To justify and explain it. You see, I see life as a kind of story. And just as a story is marred by a bad ending, so it is with life. A gradual decline followed perhaps by a long drawn-out death is a bad ending. (*Little pause*) So for me suicide is not just an impulse. Not something that needs to be sublimated or controlled, like your libido. I'm talking about rational suicide. I don't just want to kill myself. I *want* to want to kill myself. So although as an animal I have an instinct for self-preservation, as an intelligent human being I can overcome that instinct with reason.

Ronnie Oh, stop being such a philosopher.

David But that's what I am.

Ronnie Well, get on with it then and stop talking about suicide.

David But suicide's part of my philosophy. It's the ultimate philosophical problem.

Pause

Ronnie What about me?

David What?

Ronnie I need your support.

David Ah. Finally, your own naked self-interest is exposed.

Ronnie You were going to be my best man.

David I was your best man. When you married Jean.

Ronnie But you were going to be my best man when I married Melissa.

David But now you're not going to marry Melissa.

Ronnie All right, there's no need to rub it in.

David I'm sorry, Ronnie. But I'm not going to stay alive merely to be best man at a hypothetical wedding.

Ronnie Look, that's not the point. The point is, you're my best friend. I don't know what I'd do without you. I've lost Melissa. I've lost Jean. I'm about to lose my job. I don't want to lose you too.

There is a knock at the door

David (*calling*) Come in.

The door opens and Laura enters, wearing black stockings

Laura Oh.

David Hello there.

Laura Hi. Look, if I'm interrupting I'll——

Ronnie Actually, I'm just leaving. God, I'm late for the Dean. (*To David*) You're not planning anything tonight, are you?

David ...Just a good sleep. You look after yourself.

Ronnie gets up

Oh, and if you see Margaret tell her to hurry up.

Ronnie nods and goes to the door. He stops next to Laura. He looks at her legs

Ronnie Do you like Lebanese?
Laura What?
Ronnie Lebanese food. Do you like it?
Laura ...I don't think I've ever had it.
Ronnie Oh well, you must. How about dinner tonight? Say in half an hour.
I don't think I'll be longer than half an hour.
Laura Actually, I've already eaten. There was a symposium dinner.
Ronnie Fine. You could just have a drink.
Laura (*smiling*) I think I've had enough.
Ronnie ...Come for the company then?
Laura Really. No, thank you.

Ronnie nods in resignation

Ronnie I never have any luck with Americans.

Ronnie leaves

Laura He's pretty fast, isn't he?
David Yes. Sorry about that. He can't help it. He's just driven. A classic
example of Freud's theory of sexual motivation. Don't take it personally.
Laura How else am I supposed to take it?
David I mean it's not you. Actually, it's your black stockings. Ronnie has
a fetish for black stockings. If someone's wearing black stockings no
matter who it is or what she looks like, Ronnie will make a pass at her.
Laura Thanks.
David Oh, I didn't mean...
Laura I know you didn't. (*Pause*) They're tights, actually.
David Oh... I don't know that Ronnie makes a distinction.

Pause

Laura Freud later emphasised the death instinct, didn't he? But I don't think
I feel any death instinct.
David Really? Have you never, for example, stood on the edge of a station
platform looking down at the track and then, as the train approaches and

without feeling at all depressed or unhappy, felt an almost irresistible urge to jump?

Laura Yes. But I don't do it because I don't want to die.

A little pause

Doesn't death scare you?

David ...Laura, do you really want to discuss this?

Laura Yes.

David Why?

Laura ...I don't know... intellectual curiosity. (*A thought strikes her*) Think of me as a Plato to your Socrates.

He smiles

David Very well, Plato. When you say death, do you mean death or dying? As it were, the destination or the journey?

Laura Both.

He thinks

David Dying scares me a little. But that's one of the great things about suicide. If you take the appropriate precautions, you can ensure a pleasant journey. And with a bit of Dutch courage... (*He sips his whisky*)

Laura A pleasant journey?

David Yes. You can choose how, where and when to die. Instead of being the victim of chance, accident, disease or whatever, you can take control. And since death is inevitable, why leave it to luck? So much of our lives is determined by luck. I would at least like to be in control of my death. And that was my intention this morning ... before luck intervened.

Laura I see. A control freak.

David Only about my own life.

A little pause

Laura So you don't fear dying. What about death?

David The destination? What is there to fear? After all, it won't be the first time I haven't existed. Before my birth, millions of years, an eternity, passed without me. I'm not afraid of the time before my existence so why should I be afraid of the time after it? (*Little pause*) In any case, whether one is frightened by death or not, we all have to die sometime ... unless, of course, medical science can make us immortal, and I find that a far more frightening prospect.

Laura How you can be so cool about it?

David That's what philosophy is, really. Being cool about things. Even matters of life and death.

Laura But we're not just talking about matters of life and death. We're talking about your life and your death. How can you be so cool about that?

David Philosophers specialise in it. The Greeks called it *Ataraxia* … equanimity in the face of death. Think of Socrates.

Pause

Laura I'm not sure you are so cool. You just think you are. You think you're being so philosophical about suicide but you're not. What you're actually doing is hiding some, I don't know, feeling of personal failure behind a façade of philosophical commitment and justification.

David I thought you were playing Plato to my Socrates?

Laura You're just rationalising.

David I see, you've switched back to Freud.

Laura Nobody commits suicide on philosophical grounds. All that stuff about control … it's bullshit. That can't be the real reason.

David I didn't say it was. But it's a desirable side-effect.

Laura Then why?

David (*after a pause*) It's just the right time.

Laura Why is it the right time?

A little pause

David Because I've done everything I want to do, found out there wasn't much point in doing it in the first place and decided there's no reason to carry on doing it.

Laura So you do feel you've failed?

David …If you like.

Laura In your work?

David …Yes.

Laura Well, you're wrong.

David How sweet of you.

Laura And your personal life?

David Oh yes. A definite failure there.

Laura …I'm sorry.

Pause

I've been offered a job over here next year.

David (*surprised*) Congratulations.

Laura Dr Elliot, the guy running the symposium? He said he thought my paper was important.
David Really...
Laura I think that means he wants to fuck me.

A little pause

David He's a bit old for you, isn't he?
Laura Actually, I go for older men. When I was a student I dated my semantics professor.
David What went wrong?
Laura We ran out of conversation.

David laughs for a second before stopping himself

Hey, you laughed! I haven't seen you laugh before. (*Pause*) And then I moved in with my Professor of Ethics.
David How did that work out?
Laura He cheated on me.

A little pause

David I'm sorry.
Laura Yeh... I guess I have a weakness for professors. (*Little pause*) I have this tendency to eroticise the intellectual.

Pause

David Laura——
Laura Have you eaten?
David What?
Laura You haven't, have you?
David I'm not hungry.
Laura You must be starving. I'm going to fix you something.
David Please don't bother.
Laura It's no bother. And even the condemned man has a right to his last meal. Where's your kitchen?
David Really...
Laura I'll find it.

Laura goes off R

Pause. He looks at his watch. He goes over to the desk and unlocks the drawer. He opens it and takes out the revolver. He puts it on the desk and puts his hand back into the drawer. He rummages for a moment before taking out a small cardboard box about the size of a pack of cards. He opens the box and takes out a bullet. He opens the breech of the revolver and loads it. He fondles it for a moment before putting it and the bullets back in the drawer. Pause. He pours the remains of the whisky into his glass and drinks. He takes the flowers from the drinks table and throws them in the bin

> *Margaret enters*

> *They look at each other in silence for a moment*

David I've been expecting you.
Margaret David, I have to talk to you.

David holds up his hand

David Please, Margaret. Don't say another word.
Margaret But——
David Please. Just sit down. Let me speak first.

Margaret hesitates before sitting on the sofa

> Thank you. (*Pause*) You see, I know what you're going to say. You're going to try and talk me out of it, aren't you? Like Ronnie and Tom and Joanna Smart and... But it's no good, Margaret. I've made up my mind.
Margaret David——
David Please. I know this is hard for you ... but let me try and explain. I owe you that ... we've been good friends. You may have wondered why I didn't want anything more between us. Perhaps now you can understand... I needed to avoid any commitments ... any obligations. You see, I've been planning this for some time. And I've thought about it. I've thought of everything... Even the funeral arrangements. I've left instructions in my wallet for the people who did my mother. I thought they were very efficient, didn't you...? I've asked to be cremated.
Margaret David——
David I'm sorry, that was tactless. I'm not explaining myself very well. Let me try again. As you know, I lived for my work, but the book, for what it's worth, is finished ... and now that my mother's dead ... well, there's nothing. I only wish I wasn't hurting you... You look so sad. There's no need to be, I'm not sad... You'll miss me, of course, but that would be the same if I were going to live in Australia—try and think of it as going to live in ... that's a stupid thing to say. I'm just trying to keep talking because I don't want you to...

Margaret I'm pregnant.

Pause

David What?

Pause

  You can't be.
Margaret Well, I am.

Pause

David You're saying I'm the father?
Margaret Yes.
David Are you sure?
Margaret David, how many lovers do you think I had that night?

A little pause

  Please, David. You grew up without a father. You don't want your child
  to, do you?

Long pause. He picks up the empty whisky bottle and looks at it

David No... I think this calls for champagne ... don't you?

  David exits R

  Laura enters, carrying a plate of sandwiches

Laura Congratulations.

Margaret looks up

  On the baby. I couldn't help overhearing... (*She smiles*)
Margaret Who are you?
Laura I'm Laura. A friend of the Professor's. Just a friend... Oh, and by the
  way, whatever you may have heard, my information is that it's perfectly
  safe to have babies even well into middle age. Would you like a sandwich?

Tom enters

  Oh, hi there.

Tom Where's David?
Laura In the cellar. (*To Margaret*) Can I tell him?
Tom (*alarmed*) Why, what's happened?
Laura Don't look so worried. Nothing bad. (*To Margaret*) Can I tell him?
Tom Tell me what?
Margaret Go ahead.
Laura David's just heard he's going to be a daddy.
Tom (*to Margaret*) Is it true?

Margaret nods

   What did he say?
Margaret He went to get some champagne. Oh Tom. I think we may have
   won a reprieve.

They hug

Tom I'm so pleased. I'd much rather hatch and match than despatch!

They laugh. Suddenly, from off R, *there is a bang and the sound of breaking
glass. Tom and Margaret separate*

   Laura rushes off to see what's happened

   Tom and Margaret look at each other, then follow

*Pause. The phone rings. No-one answers it. It stops. We hear David's
recorded message on the answering machine as before, followed by the tone*

Bob (*on the line*) Hello, Professor. Bob here. A bit late I know, but it's just
   occurred to me that in case you're back tonight I'd better warn you I haven't
   finished your rewiring yet. After that fright you gave me I had to take the
   afternoon off. So as I said this morning—but I don't think you heard—
   don't touch that brass light switch in the cellar. It might give you a bit of
   a shock. Right then. I'll be round first thing to fix it. . . .Hope you're feeling
   better. Bye now. (*He hangs up*)

Pause

   Margaret, Laura and Tom enter

Pause

Margaret You're sure?

Laura nods

  I mean—
Laura Absolutely sure.
Margaret But what about—
Laura Believe me. I know. I learned First Aid at Berkeley. (*Pause*) There
  must have been something wrong with his connections.

Pause

Tom At least it was an accident.

Pause

Laura I think he'd rather have been in control.

Pause

Tom (*to Margaret*) And you'll have his child.
Laura That's true.

Pause

Margaret No, I won't.
Tom What?

Pause

  Oh, Margaret, you wouldn't... I mean, you couldn't...
Laura What? Of course she can.
Tom It's unthinkable.
Laura Margaret, if that's what you want——
Margaret What?
Tom That would be too awful.
Laura Don't let him bully you, Margaret. It's your choice. It's a woman's
  right.
Tom Your unborn child...
Margaret No.
Laura Attagirl!
Tom But Margaret——
Laura And if you need any counselling——
Margaret Oh shut up, will you! I'm not talking about that.

Tom and Laura are confused

Tom I don't understand.
Laura Neither do I.
Margaret The test came up negative.
Tom What?
Margaret I'm not pregnant. I thought I was but I'm not.

A short pause

Tom But ... but what about the ... you know...?
Margaret Skipped periods?
Tom Yes.
Margaret It must be the menopause.

Pause

> He would have found out eventually, of course. But I thought, while there's life— (*she breaks down*) Oh God...

Pause. Tom goes behind the desk. He rests his fingers on it

Tom Dear Lord, may his soul rest in peace, and his——
Laura Hang on. What are you doing?
Tom What am I doing?
Laura Yes. He didn't believe in God. Didn't he make that perfectly clear? He didn't believe in God, or souls, or the afterlife, or any of that stuff.

Pause

Tom No. But I do. (*Short pause*) The Lord gave and the Lord hath taken away——
Laura For God's sake! Have some respect. Don't do it here.

Pause

Tom Very well. I'll go to the chapel.

Tom leaves

Pause

Margaret Well, shouldn't we at least do something?
Laura Like what?
Margaret I don't know. Call nine-nine-nine or something?
Laura Nine-nine-nine?

Margaret Yes.
Laura Oh, you mean the emergency services?
Margaret (*getting impatient*) Yes.
Laura You see, back home it's nine-one-one——
Margaret Who cares? Let's phone them.

Laura thinks

Laura What for?
Margaret Well … for an ambulance.
Laura What's the point of an ambulance? He's dead.
Margaret All right then. Call the police.
Laura Why do we need the police? He wasn't murdered. It was an accident.
  Anyone can see that.
Margaret Well, I don't know. Call the bloody fire brigade! (*She sits down*)
Laura The only place he's going is the morgue.

Pause

  You got a car?
Margaret A car? Yes. Why?
Laura Well, there's no hurry, but we might as well take him in ourselves.
Margaret What? (*She contemplates this with alarm*)

Laura moves towards the cellar

  Where are you going?
Laura To look at him.
Margaret To look at him? Why?
Laura They say seeing someone dead helps you come to terms with it.

  Laura exits

Pause. Margaret sits and contemplates

  Ronnie enters, dishevelled and drunk, holding a half-size bottle of whisky.
  He raises it

Ronnie Bugger the lot of you. (*He drinks deeply. He slumps into the easy
  chair looking miserable*)

*Margaret doesn't seem to notice him. She is in a trance. Pause. He picks up
a sandwich and takes a bite. He glances round the room*

Where's David? (*He yawns*) Gone to bed, has he?

Margaret doesn't reply

Margaret...?

Still no reply

Oh well. (*He gets up and walks to the door*)
Margaret I'll never have a child.

Ronnie stops and considers this. He turns, opens his mouth and is about to make a proposition but then decides against it. He exits

Pause. Suddenly Laura calls out

Laura (*off*) Hey, call an ambulance!
Margaret (*waking from her trance*) What?
Laura (*off*) Call an ambulance!
Margaret (*dashing to the phone*) But you said——
Laura (*off*) For Christ's sake, call a goddam ambulance!

Margaret dials

Laura enters

What's going on? Are they coming?
Margaret It's ringing. Ah. Can I—what? (*She listens*) Damn!
Laura What?
Margaret I have to wait. They've put me in a queue. A bloody queue!
Laura Here. Let me take over. (*She takes the phone from Margaret. Into the phone*) Come on ... hurry...
Margaret (*elated*) I can't believe it!
Laura Yeh, what a country...
Margaret He's alive!
Laura What?
Margaret He's alive! You said he was dead. (*She heads for the cellar*)
Laura But Margaret. He is.

Margaret stops and turns

Margaret What?
Laura Yeh... But he's a donor! (*She shows Margaret the donor card*)

Margaret is stunned

(*Into the phone*) Hello—yes, an ambulance please. I have a dead person here who wants to donate his organs.

Life is So Peculiar plays. Margaret collapses into the easy chair as the Lights fade to Black-out. The music continues

Suicide "effect" in Act 1

A number of pin-pricks should be made in the plastic bag before putting it over the actor's head. The actor playing David in the first production also recommended hyperventilating (i.e. taking a few deep breaths) before putting the plastic bag on so as to get a store of oxygen. This procedure was advised by a doctor but safety should be ensured by taking medical advice.

FURNITURE AND PROPERTY LIST

Further dressing may be added at the director's discretion

ACT I

On stage: Heavy dark window curtains (closed)
Bookcases containing books, key under a book, stereo
Sofa
Small table. *On it:* bottle of whisky, glasses
Easy chair
Desk. *On it:* computer, telephone, answering machine, lamp, silver-framed photograph of elderly woman, open book, paper-knife. *In first drawer:* small pill bottle, transparent plastic bag, large elastic band. *In second drawer:* gun, small cardboard box holding bullets
Antique upright chair
Lamps
Phone socket
Waste bin
Light switch on wall
Key in door to flat

Off stage: Tool kit containing cloth (**Bob**)
A4-size envelope (**Laura**)
Cup of coffee (**David**)
Bag containing hand-knitted jumper (**Margaret**)
Book (**David**)
Bag containing note pad, pen, tape recorder, book (**Joanna**)

Personal: **Tom:** watch (worn throughout)
David: watch (worn throughout)

ACT II

Re-set: Photograph standing up
Phone on hook
Book in drawer

Off stage: Bag (**Margaret**)
Tray with cups, saucers, sugar, milk (**Tom**)
Towel (**David**)
Pot of tea (**Tom**)
Bunch of flowers, coat, bag containing note pad, pen, tape recorder
  (**Joanna**)
Plate of sandwiches (**Laura**)
Half-size bottle of whisky (**Ronnie**)
Donor card (**Laura**)

Personal: **David:** handkerchief

LIGHTING PLOT

Practical fittings required: various lamps, pendant light
1 Interior. The same throughout

ACT I

To open: Practicals on with covering spots

Cue 1   **David** switches off the lamps one by one   (Page 1)
        Snap off practicals and covering spots in sequence,
        reducing lighting to desk lamp only

Cue 2   **Bob** draws the curtains   (Page 3)
        Bring up general interior lighting with daylight from
        window

Cue 3   **David** draws the curtains   (Page 31)
        Reduce lighting to desk lamp only

Cue 4   **Bob** opens the door   (Page 32)
        Shaft of light through door then fade to black-out

ACT II

To open: Night effect

Cue 5   **Tom** tries to turn on the light   (Page 33)
        Flicker lighting

Cue 6   **Ronnie**: "She doesn't want to marry me."   (Page 34)
        Snap on pendant light with covering spots

Cue 7   **Tom** draws the curtains   (Page 34)
        Bring up lighting from outside

Cue 8   **Margaret** collapses into the easy chair   (Page 67)
        Fade lights

EFFECTS PLOT

ACT I

Cue 1   Before the play begins   (Page 1)
            Life is So Peculiar *plays*

Cue 2   To open   (Page 1)
            Fade music

Cue 3   **David** picks up two pills and prepares to swallow   (Page 1)
            The phone rings, continuing

Cue 4   **David** switches the answering machine on.   (Page 1)
            Cut phone ringing, bring up **David**'s *recorded message
            from the answering machine, its beep, then* **Ronnie**'s
            voice on line as script page 2

Cue 5   **David**: "Actually, Ronnie…"   (Page 3)
            Play dialling tone until **David** *hangs up*

Cue 6   **Bob** drops the tool box   (Page 32)
            Play last sequence of "Winter" from The Four Seasons

ACT II

Cue 7   To open   (Page 33)
            *Sound of rain falling, slowly dying away. After a pause,
            ring phone a few times, stop, bring up* **David**'s *answering
            machine message, its beep, then* **Ronnie**'s *voice on line
            as script page 33*

Cue 8   **Tom**: "What? . . . Ronnie? Ronnie?"   (Page 34)
            Play dialling tone until **Tom** *hangs up*

Cue 9	**Tom** tunes the radio	(Page 36)
	Bring up **Interviewer**'s *laughter and radio programme as script page 36*	
Cue 10	**David** turns the radio off	(Page 37)
	Cut radio programme	
Cue 11	**David**: "Doctors, electricians and now chaplains."	(Page 40)
	The phone rings	
Cue 12	**Tom** and **Margaret** laugh	(Page 62)
	Bang and sound of breaking glass, from off R	
Cue 13	**Tom** and **Margaret** go out	(Page 62)
	After a pause ring phone for a bit, stop, bring up **David**'s *answering machine message, its beep, then voice of* **Bob** *on line as script page 62*	
Cue 14	**Laura**: "…wants to donate his organs."	(Page 67)
	Life is So Peculiar *plays, continue to end*